Family Business
Succession:
The Final Test
of Greatness

Craig E. Aronoff, Ph.D. and
John L. Ward, Ph.D.

Family Business Leadership Series, No. 1

Family Enterprise Publishers
P.O. Box 4356
Marietta, GA 30061-4356

ISSN: 1071-5010
ISBN: 0-9651011-1-8

© 1992
Ninth Printing

Family Business Leadership Series

We believe that family businesses are special, not only to the families that own and manage them but to our society and to the private enterprise system. Having worked and interacted with hundreds of family enterprises in the past twenty years, we offer the insights of that experience and the collected wisdom of the world's best and most successful family firms.

This volume is a part of a series offering practical guidance for family businesses seeking to manage the special challenges and opportunities confronting them.

To order additional copies, contact:
   Family Enterprise Publishers
   1220-B Kennestone Circle
   Marietta, Georgia 30066
   Tel: 1-800-551-0633
   Web Site: www.efamilybusiness.com

Quantity discounts are available.

Other volumes in the series include:

Family Meetings: How to Build a Stronger Family and a Stronger Business

Another Kind of Hero: Preparing Successors For Leadership

How Families Work Together

Family Business Compensation

How to Choose & Use Advisors: Getting the Best Professional Family Business Advice

Financing Transitions: Managing Capital and Liquidity in the Family Business

Family Business Governance: Maximizing Family and Business Potential

Preparing Your Family Business For Strategic Change

Making Sibling Teams Work: The Next Generation

Developing Family Business Policies: Your Guide to the Future

Family Business Values: How to Assure a Legacy of Continuity and Success

More Than Family: Non-Family Executives in the Family Business

Contents

Tables and Exhibits

Few challenges demand more of a business owner than passing on the family business to the next generation. Family members' lifelong hopes, dreams, ambitions, relationships, even personal struggles with mortality — all figure into succession planning.

Yet succession planning is the most critical task to secure the future of private enterprise in America. Rising competition, government regulation, taxes and other problems notwithstanding, the **failure to plan for succession is the greatest current threat** to the survival of family business.

Hundreds of thousands of businesses across the nation are approaching the retirement or death of the founder with no plans for succession. No wonder fewer than one-third of family businesses survive into the second generation, and only about 13 percent make it into the third.

Business owners know the stakes are high. Ask any group of family-business people at seminars around the country to name their **Number One** concern, and the answer almost certainly will be **"succession planning."** Consider some of the issues they raise:

> *"I don't think Dad is ever going to retire. What kind of a future does this leave for me?"* — The son of a family business owner.

> *"It's impossible for me to just let go of the company I've spent a lifetime building."* — A family-business founder.

> *"I don't think I'm ever going to own any stock in the family business. What's the point in going on?"* — The daughter of a family-business owner.

> *"I don't know how I'm ever going to get along with my brothers and sisters in the business."* — One of several children in a family business.

As professional advisors often say, "Family businesses only have three problems: Succession, succession and succession."

The Final Test of Greatness

Yet succession planning can be a rich opportunity for the family business owner. Not only is it a chance to make the most of family-business assets. It is a way to perpetuate for new generations the special privileges and opportunities of ownership. And **it is a chance to create a lasting institution that will reflect the family's ideals and goals** long after the founder is gone.

For most entrepreneurs, planning for the continuity of the enterprise is the ultimate management challenge. The owner must safeguard the long-term health of the business, as well as prepare and install a successor. Other family members' roles in the business must be mapped out. If multiple siblings are involved, as they are in nearly half of all family businesses today, the headaches multiply in kind.

Plans to hold down estate taxes and ensure the founder's post-retirement security must be laid. Finally, the founder has to let go of the business he or she spent a lifetime building.

Perhaps most difficult of all, **a great succession is one hardly anybody notices. It is a non-event,** an evolutionary process arising from careful planning and artful management of expectations over a period of years. By the time the baton is finally passed, the word around the business should be, "Oh, that's what everybody expected."

To execute a smooth succession, an entrepreneur must perform heroically on many levels, both professional and personal. As management expert Peter Drucker once observed, "The final test of greatness in a CEO is how well he chooses a successor and whether he can step aside and let his successor run the company."

> *"The final test of greatness in a CEO is how well he chooses a successor and whether he can step aside and let his successor run the company"*
>
> **- Peter Drucker**

Succession: A Definition

Broadly speaking, **succession planning is a lifelong process** encompassing everything aimed at ensuring the continuity of the business through the generations. (Please see Table 1.)

If succession planning is so complex, how can the business owner break it into manageable pieces?

Most begin by laying the groundwork for transferring authority and control to the next generation. Suggestions on how to do that follow. The reader will also find information on choosing and grooming a successor, coping with the transition, communicating the change to the family and the organization and, perhaps most difficult of all, letting go gracefully.

We make an important assumption: that the owner already has decided to keep the business in the family. This isn't a decision to be taken lightly. It requires serious reflection and a strong commitment by the owner-manager and other family members.

We also assume that a successor candidate exists within the family, although succession planning should be given just as much careful attention in businesses where only non-family candidates are available.

The Rewards of Succession Planning

It was hardly a typical father-son argument. The setting was a gathering of family-business owners. The father, founder of a gasoline and convenience-store chain, was debating with his successor.

"I owe more to my son than my son owes to me," the father told a listener.

"No, I owe more to you," the son said.

"What did I create all this for? You're the one who is going to sustain it and grow this legacy," the father said.

"But you're the one who has given me the opportunity," the son replied.

Many business owners hope as they grow older to accomplish more than just survival. **They desire a kind of immortality** — to create

TABLE 1

> ## PLANNING FOR BUSINESS CONTINUITY: A CHECKLIST
>
> - ☐ Develop children's values and capabilities
> - ☐ Create lifelong financial security for parents
> - ☐ Finalize the family's mission statement
> - ☐ Finalize the owners' estate plan
> - ☐ Finalize the business's strategic plan
> - ☐ Select a successor
> - ☐ Plan successor's personal development
> - ☐ Map career paths for other family members
> - ☐ Transfer ownership and control
> - ☐ Build a family team of owners
> - ☐ Write participation policy for family members
> - ☐ Retain non-family managers
> - ☐ Install outside directors
> - ☐ Prepare for retirement
> - ☐ Prepare contingency plan for succession in crisis
> - ☐ Develop a new management team

something significant and strong enough to endure beyond their lifetime.

Many of these entrepreneurs find succession planning opens doors to that goal. It enables them to pass on to subsequent generations some of the rewards of entrepreneurship — the opportunity to manage capital, to make things happen in the community and to have a sense of control over one's destiny.

A family business that thrives through successive generations affords the family a special forum to express individual creativity. Family members can learn the value of shared decision-making and working toward common goals. All of this heightens the entrepreneur's impact and magnifies the benefits of his or her years of hard work.

Good succession planning also enhances the value of the business by retaining the most talented potential successors. Too often, the best candidates flee out of frustration over succession prospects, seeking brighter opportunities elsewhere. Some families encourage this, maintaining the business so "the children who can't take care of themselves will have something to do." Over time, this practice destroys the integrity of the business.

Successors' frustration can erupt into the kind of family clash that one business owner experienced as he neared retirement age. This father stubbornly refused to discuss succession issues with his two sons. "I'm never going to retire," he told them. "You guys can work it out after I'm dead."

But when the three men travelled together to an out-of-town sales meeting, the sons seized the initiative — by kidnapping their father. When the company plane took off, they told the father the plane wouldn't land until he agreed to do some succession planning. Then, they diverted the flight to the home of a waiting consultant, who was prepared to help begin the process.

Revitalizing strategy. A well-managed succession also brings a fresh perspective to management that can revitalize strategy.

The son of a Savannah, Ga., retailing family was studying for his MBA in Atlanta when a stroll through a discount store sparked an idea. The discounter's market was similar to the one served by his family's modest retail store, which specialized in cosmetics for blacks. Yet nowhere on the discounter's shelves were any ethnic products.

The young man contacted the store's management and asked for a couple of feet of shelf space for ethnic cosmetics. The discount chain agreed to offer the products in four stores, and sales boomed. Today, the son is the owner of Ben Sheftall Distributing Company, Inc., a rapidly expanding ethnic-cosmetics company with a $50-million-a-year wholesaling operation.

The entrepreneurial energy of successors driving the business built by their parents and grandparents can create a powerful business. Such was the pattern in one coffee-distribution company when two brothers in the third generation of family management grew restless. "If we're distributing coffee, why aren't we distributing tea?" they wondered. In a series of adroit strategic moves, the brothers produced enough private-label teabags to build the nation's second largest tea packer.

Good succession planning also enhances the value of the business

The Succession Conspiracy

Despite the rewards of succession planning, **many family-business owners find it easier to live with ambiguity**. Who enjoys thinking about death or disability, making choices among children, and letting go of a powerful, prestigious, secure position for an uncertain future?

In what Yale University's Dr. Ivan Lansberg calls "the succession conspiracy," everyone involved may conclude it is in his or her best interests to avoid the issue altogether. Many entrepreneurs resist succession planning as a troublesome admission of mortality. Doing it means admitting that you won't live forever — a step they feel diminishes them.

Spouses aren't usually eager to bring up the subject of retirement or death. Children don't want to be considered greedy or pushy, and they also may have difficulty facing the prospect of their parents' passing.

Key managers resist rocking the boat. Disrupting their own relationships with the founder in favor of a new, untested boss is unappealing. Friends and advisors hesitate to raise the subject, for fear of offending the owner or hurting feelings.

Our culture offers few helpful models. Most heroes are thought of as "dying with their boots on" rather than stepping aside gracefully.

Dodging the issue protects business owners from making the tough decisions involved in succession planning. They tell themselves that by avoiding the issue, they are retaining key people in the business who might leave if a successor were named.

These leaders are kidding themselves. Avoiding the topic doesn't mean succession will never happen, and key people in the business know that. As mentioned earlier, a lack of planning may actually encourage them to depart for a company with a better planned future. Like the many other people who depend on a healthy family business — family, employees, suppliers, customers and the community — key executives invariably respect the business owner's courage in preparing for a new generation of management. They hope for no less from a corporate leader. In this sense, **succession planning is the cornerstone of stewardship**.

Nevertheless, some founders continue to avoid the issue in a kind of final, unconscious demand for the loyalty of all those who depend on the business: "How can you lack faith in me after all I have done for you? Just trust me."

If the untimely death or disability of the CEO pierces the fog, it becomes clear that he or she has unwittingly created a time bomb. The surviving owners or heirs may be disoriented and ill-prepared for management. No plans have been laid. The whole family avoided all the sensitive issues while Mom or Dad was alive.

Yet the **silence has not prevented each family member from forming his or her own private expectations** about dividends, compensation of management, family participation in the business and rights to ownership. If worse comes to worst, each soon hires a lawyer, the first step into a litigious quagmire that can destroy everything the parents built over a lifetime.

Dr. Léon Danco, a respected family-business consultant, assesses the risk: "If you don't plan, you'll have the satisfaction of knowing that it's the lawyers four limousines back who will be settling your family's future."

Even in peaceful families, a poorly planned succession is costly. Key employees may leave if they lack confidence in the new CEO. Estate taxes will drain capital. If the business is sold, an absence of consistent, strong management will reduce the price, eroding the assets that have taken a lifetime to build.

Succession planning is the cornerstone of stewardship.

How the CEO Should Prepare

The attitude of the business owner is the single most important factor in any succession.

But preparing for succession often brings the founder face-to-face with some daunting personal obstacles.

He or she must face the possibility of feeling rivalry with a successor. **Seeing younger family members make their own mark on the business can be a bittersweet experience.** It is tough to resist taking credit for their accomplishments or feeling like a failure if successors do too well.

The founder must begin to separate his or her personal identity from the business. This is especially hard for those who have spent their lives viewing the business as an extension of themselves. "Without me, this company isn't worth anything," they may think proudly.

Now, often for the first time, the founder must begin to consider questions like: What is the value of this business, apart from me? How can I communicate what I do to a new generation of management? How do I move functions to other people? How can I pass on my skills? How do I transfer my business relationships?

As if that weren't hard enough, the business owner must prepare to let go of power. And he or she must confront mortality, in a real and compelling way.

A New Kind of Goal. This long, subtle process often adds a new dimension to the entrepreneur's business experience.

After years of striving for the "home run" — the heroic masterstroke that snares the big contract, lands the promising recruit or captures the new market — the entrepreneur hardly knows how to savor the more subtle rewards of succession planning.

In fact, the well-planned succession is more like the graceful exchange of the baton between runners in a relay race. Like the handoff, **the leadership transfer is almost undetectable to the spectator.** Yet it requires stamina, discipline, conditioning and shared goals. It also demands a measure of artistry — the teamwork required to pass the baton smoothly at full speed, with the runners neither missing a stride nor stumbling over each other as they pass.

Laying the Foundation. Skills of this sort require years of step-by-step practice.

One of the first steps is to lay the foundation for a succession plan. **Long before succession, the founder should write a strategic plan and personal financial and estate plan.** The family also should prepare a family mission statement reflecting its resolve to continue the enterprise as a family-owned operation. (Please see Table 2.)

TABLE 2

THE FIRST STEPS TO SUCCESSION PLANNING

1. Business Strategic Plan
2. Founder's Personal Financial Plan
3. Family's Mission Statement
4. Owner's Estate Plan

Many business owners call on professional advisors or outside directors to help with these plans. But briefly, the strategic plan will help identify the qualities needed in the business's future leadership — the strategic mandate. Managing a more diverse work force, coping with an increasingly international economy, managing risk from volatile financial markets — all are abilities that may be even more helpful in the future. Team-building skills and a sense of stewardship of family assets are also especially important for CEOs of family businesses beyond the first generation.

The personal financial and estate plans should safeguard assets from taxes and ensure the parents' security after retirement. Few thoughts are more unnerving to an entrepreneur than the idea of dependence on a business in the hands of an unproven successor. **Parents need a secure source of income, preferably separate from the business,** to provide post-retirement comfort and confidence.

For full leadership and ownership succession to take place, the departing parents must believe themselves personally financially secure — as independent as possible of the business for the rest of their lives. The parent-owners of a small suburban weekly newspaper chain outlined their plan as seen in Exhibit 1:

EXHIBIT 1 ███████████████████████████████

One Founder's Plan for Personal Financial Security

Goals
- *Lifetime annual income of $200,000 per year*
- *Liquid asset "security blanket" of $1,000,000*

Means
- *Long-term lease on business real estate of $100,000 per year*
- *8 percent annual income on $1,250,000 of liquid assets for $100,000 per year*

Plans for Amassing $1.25 Million Private Capital
- *Extra "bonus" compensation of $150,000 per year for four years*
- *Sale of some stock back to company for approximately $625,000 (that the business borrows from the bank) after four years*

The Family's Resolve. A crucial factor in the outcome of any succession effort is the resolve to continue the business as a family-owned enterprise.

A family mission statement articulates the family's commitment and the reasons behind it. It also describes other aspects of the family's vision for the business and the family role in it. Some family mission statements are brief, contained in a few succinct sentences or paragraphs. Others may continue for several pages, including, among other things:

- A statement of family values as they relate to the business
- Policies on family participation in the business
- Principles guiding family-member compensation
- Guidelines for family-member advancement in the business
- A family code of conduct as it relates to the business
- Policies on sharing financial information
- Guidelines for forming a family organization.

Exhibit 2 contains an example of a family mission statement.

EXHIBIT 2 ▰▰▰▰▰▰▰▰▰▰▰▰▰▰▰▰▰▰▰▰▰▰▰

A Family Mission Statement

"We are fortunate to have a privately owned business in our family. The business provides family members opportunities that are difficult to replicate: opportunities to earn financial independence, to learn the skills of business and leadership, to contribute actively to others in the community, and to share in common family interests. To work productively is to grow, to respect humility, to know the realities of life. Not to work is an unhealthy state. Maintaining the business in the family and seeking to expand and strengthen the business will help assure that our family will have productive work rather than live off the accomplishments of past generations. We are committed to the long-term success of our family business for the benefit of our future generations.

The business must be run as a business. In that way family members will know that they have earned their personal successes; those that work for us will know that their careers and families will be secure. It is not easy to run a family business like a business. Family members will inevitably have needs and turn to the business to fill them. For that reason we, as a family, have all openly pledged to help one another when one is in need from our personal resources — not from those of the business. We have provided an estate apart from the business to assure some comfort and security for each family member; we hope family members will forever prolong the prudence our family has always practiced by saving these funds rather than spending them.

All family members are welcome in the business. We are fortunate to be a large enough business to have ample opportunities. As in the past, however, family members may be asked to withdraw if their contributions and business circumstances so require.

We hope one of more family members will qualify to be able future leaders of the business. For our business that will require excellent skills and excellent educational backgrounds. We wish a family member to serve as chief executive and to assume the traditions of our business and family, as well as ensure by example that it remains a working business for the family — not a passive investment.

To help ensure that the family acts as one and works hard to formulate common plans and ideals, we have established a voting trust. Three members of the family will be elected as trustees for three-year terms —

one each year. No family member may serve as trustee for more than two consecutive terms. The trust will represent the family shareholders.

Business decisions will be aided by a board of directors comprised of the three trustees and four others who are neither family members nor employees. If we are to run ourselves like a business, we should be able to convince the outside directors of the rightness of our business plans and goals.

The trustees will also accept informal roles as family leaders. In that position they will be available to help any family member in need or to counsel family members on matters of financial orientation. The trustees will help identify investment opportunities for all family members to share in (voluntarily). These non-family business investments will provide one form of common family interests.

Individual family members may suggest any agenda item to the trustees on a confidential basis. The trustees will make every effort to examine and resolve family differences.

In the end, this plan is no stronger than the will and love of the entire family. Together we can provide great opportunities for ourselves and our children and even their children. It has been done before. Surely we can do it now. Why not?"

Meeting with family members to prepare this statement can help all involved understand the reasons for completing the succession process, long before the transfer of authority and control actually takes place.

A Team Approach. The founder, a unique individual who has played many roles in the business, also may choose to begin cultivating a team approach to top management. This can help prepare the organization for his or her departure.

This may entail creating positions in top management nearly equal in importance and pay to the CEO. The entire top management team should be analyzed for the skills, values and knowledge required by the competitive environment. Then, the CEO should list current responsibilities and key relationships and lay plans for shifting them to others.

Post-Retirement Activities. Founders who enjoy the most success in passing on the business tend to begin seeking new post-retirement endeavors as early as their late forties or early fifties. Many eagerly anticipate their successors' taking over so they can begin teaching, consulting, writing, building a charitable foundation, forming a new business or other activities.

Entrepreneurs who find a new focus for their energies are giving a great gift to their heirs: a clean and healthy break with the business, so that it can continue under the leadership of a new generation. Affirmative answers to the questions in the "Letting Go" checklist are critical to the ability to accomplish this. (Please see Table 3.)

TABLE 3

THE OWNER-MANAGER'S "LETTING-GO" CHECKLIST

☐ Am I committed to family succession? Is it a dream I deeply feel?

☐ Will my spouse and I be financially secure after retirement?

☐ Have I chosen a successor and set a firm date to retire?

☐ Do I believe there is life after retirement?

☐ Does an absorbing new challenge or interest await me after retirement?

☐ Am I able to delegate decisions and authority?

☐ Am I willing to let others take new business risks?

☐ Do I trust key people with company financial information?

When to Start

While venture capitalists are not always the best friends of family business, they have a useful rule of thumb:

As soon as you get involved in any deal, start working on an exit strategy.

Thinking early about exit strategies is sensible — not only in capital planning, but for management and ownership succession as well. **The first night you sleep well as a business owner, satisfied that you have a viable company, is the signal to begin thinking about the continuity of the enterprise.**

Contingency Planning. The possibility of the untimely death or disability of the CEO looms as a major threat to family businesses.

Many owners install an outside board of directors or advisors as an "insurance policy" for their spouse or family, to help with a transition to new leadership if necessary. Unlike key managers, lenders, professional advisors and others, outside directors have no vested interest in the outcome of emergency leadership succession. Their interest is in the welfare of the business and the family.

If a successor has been chosen, he or she may be forced to act like an entrepreneur, assuming leadership quickly and doing what is necessary to sustain the business. Again, the counsel of an outside board can be invaluable.

Whatever the case, contingency plans for succession are a crucial safeguard against untimely forced sale or liquidation of the business.

Planning for Succession. While succession planning done well is a lifelong process, most of the work of preparing for the transfer of authority and control can be done in five to fifteen years. Most owners begin thinking about succession in earnest at about 45 to 50 years of age, with plans to retire at about 60 to 65. Typically, their children would be 25 or 30, with their formal education and outside work experience behind them.

Beginning succession planning at this stage allows the 15 years needed to make a choice among multiple candidates. It allows time to develop and groom potential successors, to give them a chance to demonstrate their abilities and to pull together a family executive committee or succession task force to help.

The third-generation CEO of one successful steel-distributing concern is preparing for succession even though, at 54, he is years from retirement. With five third-generation owners in the business and several of their children waiting in the wings, it isn't clear who will be candidates to succeed him.

The CEO has begun developing criteria for a successor, building an outside board, professionalizing management and making other changes to smooth the transfer of power when the time comes. By the time succession actually takes place, the process will be well understood and the likelihood of conflict reduced.

Once a successor has been chosen, five years is usually enough to permit training and testing of the heir apparent and to execute a smooth leadership transition.

Many owners install an outside board of directors or advisors as an "insurance policy" for their spouse or family

The Elements of a Succession Plan

The backbone of any succession effort is a good plan.

This document — prepared by the CEO (often with the help of a professional advisor or outside directors) or by a company task force charged with succession — is a guide to managing all the issues that are likely to surface during this period.

It should reflect careful forethought about several key aspects of succession:

- A personal development plan for the successor.

- Leadership development for the successor.

- The process for choosing a successor.

- The evolving leadership roles of founder and successor, including job descriptions at various stages for both.

- A plan to communicate the succession decision to the family, the company and the community.

- A plan for organizational succession, covering evolution of top management and the board, career paths for key managers, and future family participation in the business.

Once complete, the succession plan should be reviewed annually with an eye to the contingencies that could render it useless. What if a key person dies or is disabled? What if a major shareholder leaves the business? What happens in the event of a divorce, marriage or remarriage of a family shareholder?

Let's take a closer look at each of the major facets of an effective succession plan.

A Personal Development Plan for the Successor. For many entrepreneurs, developing children into effective successors is more difficult than building a new business.

Parents lay the groundwork for succession while their children are small. The values taught then — hard work, saving, investing, sharing, settling disputes peacefully and so on — help foster smooth succession, as well as good family relationships.

The signals you send in talking about the business at home instill attitudes in your children that last a lifetime.

Many family-business heirs hear nothing but complaints when the business owner comes home from the office. The suppliers sent the wrong order, the bank is demanding more money, two people quit and customers aren't paying their bills on time.

"Sometimes I'd like to chuck it all!" Dad grumbles. Then he turns to his son or daughter and promises, "Some day this will all be yours!" No wonder the child shrinks in dismay.

If passing on the family business to your children is your hope, begin early to present a balanced perspective on the joys and sorrows of entrepreneurship. Talk about the rewards as well as the headaches.

An Option — Not an Obligation. Parents should talk about the family business as a career opportunity for their children, not an obligation.

Children should not be led to believe early that the business is theirs, no matter what. On the other hand, there is no reason for the owner to deceive anyone about his or her hope that management will remain in the family.

"If at some point you become interested in the family business, you will be very welcome. But it's only one of your many options," parents might say. "We will support and encourage you no matter what you decide."

Attitude Preparation. Too many family-business heirs approach their work with the attitude, "Gee, I like to do this or that. Why don't you set up a subsidiary so I can do it?"

Once successors have decided to enter the business, they should be encouraged to think of the future in terms of making the **greatest possible contribution** — not reaping the greatest possible benefits. This dispels the notion that entering the family business is a birthright, regardless of the talents or attitude of the recipient.

The Personal Development Phase. A personal development program should be planned early for the successor candidate. An example of one company's development program for each of its family candidates for succession is contained in Exhibit 3.

The heir apparent should be encouraged while in his or her 20s to get three to five years of outside work experience, preferably in a larger company. This fosters new skills, fresh ideas and self-confidence, making the successor feel as though he or she is in the family business by choice — not because he or

Parents lay the groundwork for succession while their children are small.

18

she couldn't make it anywhere else. Outside work helps successors learn about the job market and their own market value. They also discover that "the grass isn't always greener" away from the family business.

Successor candidates also should be encouraged to develop skills complementary to those of the founder or other family members in the business. If the boss dislikes recordkeeping, for instance, the successor might develop expertise in accounting and data processing. If other key family members love the production end of the business but dislike "people problems," the successor candidate might emphasize professional employee-development skills. This approach ensures that the next generation will contribute something new, and also can reduce the likelihood of conflict between the founder and successor.

EXHIBIT 3 ███████████████████████████████████

A Development Program for Successor Candidates

Here is how one company approached the task of successor development:

"We will consider several types of development opportunities for each of the family candidates for succession:

- Matching with mentors (managers or consultants)
- Outside exposure (peer groups such as the Young Presidents' Organization, visits to other companies)
- Industry education
- Team-building (task forces, Outward Bound, joint travel)
- Rotation and cross-training
- Involvement in business processes (board meetings, strategic planning meetings, company socials and ceremonies, etc.)
- Information flow
- Peer associations outside the firm
- Autonomous P & L responsibility.

We will also identify specific job situations that offer special developmental opportunities. The best, so far, are sales manager for the eastern territory and warehouse manager for the new locations."

When the successor candidate enters the family business, he or she should be hired into an existing job. This helps determine pay and performance standards. It also allays resentment among employees who may doubt the successor's qualifications.

The successor should also have an opportunity to learn from a mentor outside the family — a valued and loyal employee, an outside director, a family friend or advisor, or managers in a similar family-owned business.

The owner-manager or mentor should take pains to teach the successor the company's history, strategy, philosophy and culture, so the candidate can grasp the underlying principles that hold the enterprise together. Understanding the foundation of the business is crucial to the successor's future ability to bring about change.

Leadership Development for the Successor. Once a probable successor is chosen, he or she should begin a more formal program of leadership development. Ideally, this happens as the candidate approaches 30 or 35 and the person in power nears the mid-50s.

Succession planners should map out a career path through areas where the successor needs training — operations, marketing, strategy, and so on. Performance standards for the successor should be written and regular evaluations should be planned.

The successor should have the opportunity to run a visible area of the business, such as supervising a department or handling advertising. As the candidate gains experience, he or she usually receives greater responsibility, including running a profit center.

Successors should also be encouraged to learn useful skills and values outside the business. Many join peer groups of successors to share experiences and lend support. The Executive Committee, in San Diego, or the Young Presidents Organization, a New York-based group of CEOs in their 30s or 40s, are two such groups. Others form informal support groups of their own. All the while, the successor is being regularly evaluated, and a mentor is coaching the successor in needed areas.

A Personal Rationale. Successors in family businesses have a tough role. They often can not fulfill their parent's expectations because they are not like their parent. Some have trouble making their own mark on the business, particularly if the founder is insecure in any way.

At some point, most question their commitment to the family business. "What am I doing here?" they may wonder. "I'm smart. I had alternatives. Now I'm getting beat up by Dad (or things aren't working as smoothly as I want, or the family is complaining about my treatment of them). What's the point?"

Succession planners should try to help the successor develop a personal rationale for staying in the business. Why do you see this as an opportunity? Why is this work important to you? Encouraging the successor to answer these questions thoughtfully early in the succession process can be of tremendous help later, when the going gets tough.

Often successors experience at some point a feeling of directionlessness. Although they have worked long and hard to earn responsibility and authority, a sense of mastery eludes them. "There seems to be one final step I'm missing, and Dad won't tell me what it is!" they complain.

True achievement can't be found by following a map drawn by others. Dr. David Livingston, the famed British explorer of Africa, received many offers of help in his work as a medical missionary from philanthropic groups in England. "Dr. Livingston," one group wrote, "We have many good young men who would like to serve with you. Have you cut a road through the jungle so they can reach you?"

"If they're the kind of men who need a road through the jungle," Dr. Livingston wrote back, "then I can't use them."

Often, the founder's message is similar. Once the successor assumes control of the business, Dad or Mom won't be there to make suggestions or give advice. Late in the succession process, the founder may begin to test the successor's ability to make decisions unaided — to carve his or her own path through the jungle.

If the successor meets all these challenges well, he or she is ready to begin the transition to leadership. (Some criteria for successor development are listed in Table 4.)

The Process of Choosing a Successor. One of the biggest barriers to succession planning is parents' reluctance to choose among their children.

"I don't want to face this issue because I'm going to lose either way," parents may think. "Even if I'm right in my selection, I lose. I would violate all family rules by picking one of my kids as a favorite, or more intelligent, capable, powerful or trusted."

More parents face this dilemma today than ever before. **Nearly 50 percent of all family businesses now employ multiple offspring,** compared with 20 percent just

Nearly 50 percent of all family businesses now employ multiple offspring

a few years ago, according to recent surveys. **Traditions such as handing the business to the oldest son or barring women from the business are crumbling.**

Young people's interest in working in family businesses is growing fast. Family values and relationships are stirring renewed popular interest. Many family businesses have professionalized management, increasing their appeal. Diminished career opportunities in big corporations and in overcrowded professions, such as law, have speeded the trend.

With so many family businesses eventually co-owned or co-managed by several offspring, succession issues become even more complex. Despite the widespread conviction that a business needs a single leader, a surprising number of family businesses today are managed by committee. Nordstrom Inc., the big family-run retailer based in Seattle, recently

TABLE 4 _____

CHECKLIST FOR
SUCCESSOR DEVELOPMENT

☐ Has the successor gained worthwhile experience outside the family business?

☐ Has a clear personal development plan been laid for the successor?

☐ Is someone other than a parent teaching and mentoring the successor?

☐ Does the successor have an opportunity to make an independent and visible contribution to the business?

☐ Is the successor continuing to learn useful skills and values outside the business, as well as inside?

☐ Is the owner-manager continually teaching the successor the business history, philosophy and strategy?

☐ Does the successor have opportunities outside the business to exercise leadership and gain respect?

☐ Has the successor developed a personal rationale for working in the business, one that will provide a sense of purpose when times get tough?

☐ Does the successor spend time with other family business successors, sharing interests and concerns?

named four key executives to a new Office of the President, reporting to a four-person Office of the Chairman composed of Nordstrom family members.

Other family businesses stick to a more traditional structure with a single CEO. This raises questions about how a choice should be made among multiple offspring.

A successor can be chosen in several ways. Some business owners bite the bullet and make a choice, either very early or after a period of competition. Others delegate the decision to a board of outside directors or to a management committee of family members. In a nearly ideal solution, still others manage to attain consensus among family members, directors and key executives.

Let's take a closer look at the pros and cons of these alternatives.

Early Selection. Some business owners choose among potential successors very early, often while the oldest children are still in their 20s. This method tends to work best in families whose offspring are very different in age or capability.

Parents who choose early may want to reassure everyone that they intend the business to continue under family ownership. Parents are still young enough to heal any wounds inflicted by their choice. They also want to give other family members who weren't chosen time to pursue alternate career paths if they want.

An early choice reduces the risk that unexpected death or disability of the founder will leave the business drifting. It also erases the possibility that deciding will become more difficult as the founder and children grow older.

This method can eliminate talented younger children from the running too early, though. It forces selection of a CEO long before the future strategic needs of the business have become clear. It also requires parents to make difficult choices and risks causing hard feelings among family members.

Competition Over Time. Some founders allow candidates to compete for leadership over time. This reduces the risk of making the wrong choice. It allows time for the business's strategic needs to influence the selection.

Unfortunately, this method sometimes becomes an excuse not to decide. It increases the risk that no successor will be chosen in time. And **making a choice becomes more difficult as children grow older.** Candidates may grow resentful as their positions shift over time. "It used to be clear that I was the logical candidate, but now it looks as though you're not going to pick anyone!" they may say. And as the owners approach retirement, their parental values may grow more important to them, making a choice among their children even more difficult.

The Outside Board as Catalyst. Many parents seek outside help with succession. The founder may ask the company's board of directors to help design the selection process, create a succession plan and oversee implementation. Directors can also help prepare and counsel family members involved in the process.

Some family businesses actually assemble an active board of outside directors or advisors for the first time primarily to help with succession. Ideally, the board is composed of respected peers of the CEO who can act as a sounding board and help mentor the successor. Directors can be an invaluable source of stability and cohesiveness at difficult times in the succession process.

The Family Executive Team. Some parents assign responsibility for succession to an executive committee or task force of siblings in the business. This removes the burden of a decision from parents and encourages consensus among brothers and sisters. As this group works together, **an obvious leader sometimes emerges.** "It's clear Mary wants this more than anyone else. She puts in the time and tries to bring us together," family members may conclude.

This method can end in stalemate, though. It also risks encouraging politicking and the formation of emotional alliances that can hurt the business and the family.

Another possibility is that the siblings will decide not to decide, but to take on leadership of the business as a team. This may clash with the views of the founder and others that a business should be run as a hierarchy with a single head. It also means that the leadership of the business is no stronger than the consensus of the siblings on the management team.

Once responsibility has been given to the sibling task force, however, it is difficult to override its decision.

The Non-Family CEO. Some business owners name a non-family CEO and ask that person to pick a successor. This method removes the burden of choice from the parents and can be used to fill a management gap if the founder retires before any family successors are ready.

This method is risky, though, especially if the non-family CEO has sole responsibility. Non-family executives can be even more vulnerable to family politicking and worries about showing favoritism than family

24

executives. They may fear a stockholder revolt. They also may lack understanding of the business's values, history and culture to guide their choice. The non-family executive in this situation is especially in need of support and oversight by an outside board.

The Professional Advisor. Some family businesses leave the choice to a paid advisor such as a lawyer, industrial psychologist or family-business consultant. This method has many of the same risks as asking a non-family CEO to make the choice. Also, it is typically used after the founder has died — far too late for planning and preparation.

Selection by Default. Some parents let time pass until most of the successor candidates have left the business for greener pastures. This makes the choice obvious. "The person who has waited longest deserves the job," these owners reason.

Unfortunately, this method tends to chase away the most ambitious, eager and talented candidates, leaving the least qualified candidate to take the helm. Also, there is no guarantee that retirement, death or disability of the founder won't occur before the choice has been made.

Consensus Among Family, Board and Executives. Ideally, the business owner, family members, directors and the executive team can agree on criteria, a selection process and a timetable for succession. Once this is achieved, a leading candidate tends to emerge over time with a minimum of conflict. Either the board or the family executive team can then act as a catalyst for a final decision.

This process of "evolutionary self-revelation" is a little like the creation of improvisational comedy. The players all operate according to a few principles: They have to involve a certain number of actors, finish in a certain length of time, incorporate ideas from the audience, and so on. Yet none of the players knows as the act begins how it will end. The outcome each night is unique, a product of the combined talents of the players and input from the audience. It becomes obvious to the players only after the performance is well underway.

Similarly, **a well-planned family-business succession is neither random nor choreographed.** The people involved are governed by certain principles or procedures — that a successor will be chosen within five years, for instance, and then only by consensus of the

A well-planned family-business succession is neither random nor choreographed

board and key family members. But no one knows as the process begins who will be selected. Instead, the choice becomes apparent over time. "Charlie is working hardest to bring us together," family members may conclude. Or, "Susan's success at moving her profit center into new areas shows that she is the best leader." Ideally, this approach unburdens parents and leads to deliberate, well-reasoned choices with less room for rancor within the family.

The Succession Task Force. Larger, older companies with formal boards and organized family councils sometimes use the succession task force, a more formal version of the consensus method described above. Key managers, family members and directors make up the task force. The group may decide on a succession plan and a selection process, then monitor its implementation. Such a task force can also help with other aspects of succession, including compensation of key family and non-family managers, job descriptions and team-building.

While small to medium-sized family businesses typically use less formal methods, companies in the third generation of family management or beyond often use an outside board or succession task force to select a successor.

No Logical Candidate. In some family businesses, it becomes clear during the preparation or planning process that no logical successor candidate exists within the family. An outside board or professional advisor can be helpful in considering another route to succession or other alternatives.

At some point, all owners should at least consider alternatives to family succession, including naming a non-family successor. This guards against the possibility that none of the children will work out as successors, or that all might decide to pursue other interests.

The Evolving Leadership Roles of Founder and Successor. No athlete, no matter how swift or skilled, would enter a relay race without first practicing the transfer of the baton.

Step by step, the runner learns the graceful exchange needed to accept the responsibility of team leadership from another.

The same is true of the family-business successor. Once designated, he or she must practice the skills of leadership. By the time the founder and successor pass the baton, they complete the transfer at full speed. The result: a continuity that sustains the team's overall momentum while bringing new energy and power to the race.

Much is at stake. If the handoff goes poorly, with one runner clinging to the baton or the other fumbling it, the race is lost. A successor may resign or be dismissed, casting a shadow on the family and the future of the business.

Many family businesses make a mistake at this stage. Often, the heir apparent is given a broad title such as executive vice president, asked to learn as much as possible about the business, and left to drift without assuming authority over anything. Then at his or her "coronation," all the responsibility suddenly is handed over, and the successor is expected to begin running at full speed.

A better method is to give the successor new responsibilities one by one, in a phased transition that is clear to everyone involved. Five years before the successor takes control of operations as president, he or she might be given responsibility for sales and marketing. Two years later, production or operations is added. In another year, the successor may take on finance and administration.

Ideally, the founder is less and less involved in decision-making during this period. Early in the process, each of the successor's decisions may require parental involvement and approval. Next, the parent may be asked for concurrence after a decision has been made. Then the parent is only informed of decisions after the fact. Finally, the successor seeks the parent's counsel only when needed, as though the founder were a consultant on call.

One successor describes this period as a process of "finding inner confidence." The first year after he assumed the role of general manager, he recalls, "I'd call Dad almost daily to ask him about just about everything." By the second year, he picked up the phone only on Tuesdays and Thursdays. If his father was out, he'd always get back to him by the next day.

By the third year, "I'd call on Tuesdays, and he'd call back sometimes a week later. Sometimes I'd just forget to call him on some things. By then, we realized that the transition was complete."

Important business relationships need to be transferred to the new leader, too. The CEO should at some point list key people — advisors, suppliers, customers and others — and introduce each to the successor so that new relationships can be formed.

Taking the Helm. When the successor finally becomes president, he or she should be given broad authority for all areas not specifically assigned to the founder, who typically becomes chairman.

The chairman keeps responsibility only for a list of clearly defined functions traditionally reserved for the board: dividends, approving a capital budget, debt levels, acquisitions and divestitures, and hiring, firing and compensation of officers.

This retains the founder's control over such sensitive decisions as firing a veteran manager, setting family members' salaries or selling key operations. But it gives management freedom to the successor, who needs latitude at this stage to begin running the business and meeting strategic goals in his or her own way.

Clear job descriptions for both the successor and the founder at all stages are crucial in staying the course and preventing misunderstandings and mistrust among employees.

Finally, the transition has to end. The founder must surrender authority, preferably by an agreed-upon date. Usually, the transfer of ownership control follows.

Letting Go Gracefully. Few statements irritate a successor more than a parent's saying, "I'm retired — more or less."

Founders often like it that way. They can lead a life of leisure, when they feel like it. They can drop in on the business and "straighten things out" when they feel like it, too. They have the best of both worlds.

But all the while, the successor may be biting his or her lip to contain anger. The successor is eager to lead the business. But how is he or she to know whether the founder is more or less in control at any given time? How would you feel as CEO if your authority was open to question at any time, without notice?

Imagine the consequences in a relay race if the runner passing the baton doesn't get out of the way: a stumble or a collision, a dropped baton or even permanent injury to the athletes.

And if the baton is passed too late, all is lost — including the race. In one family business, a 91-year-old founder delegated check-signing authority to his 64-year-old son only because his hand was shaking too badly to write. In another, a third-generation family-business manager, at 58, was eagerly anticipating retirement — well before his 79-year-old father had even thought of it. These malingering elders are wasting potential, not only of the younger generation but probably of the business itself.

Owners need to establish a firm deadline for transferring power. A board of outside directors or advisors can help them stick to the schedule.

Few statements irritate a successor more than a parent's saying, "I'm retired — more or less."

The Hurdles. Letting go is a complex and difficult process. As discussed above and again at greater length below, planning for your post-retirement financial security can eliminate one source of apprehension. Unless you are financially independent, you won't be able to resist the temptation of interfering with the business.

Many business owners also fear a loss of personal identity or a sense of boredom or uselessness. "I know three people who died the day after they retired!" the founder may recall. **Founders who lack other interests, or whose parents had a brief or unhappy retirement, are most likely to have trouble.**

As successors gradually assume more authority, parents can begin new activities just as gradually. Most entrepreneurs find they need more than just recreation and leisure — they need responsibility for leadership and development of something new, as discussed below.

The founder above all should avoid returning to the business after the leadership transition is complete. Many entrepreneurs are tempted to do this two to five years after retirement, especially if they keep voting stock control. This move almost always seriously damages family relationships, and the presence of two "leaders" has a devastating effect on the business as well. As a safeguard, the founder should relinquish voting stock control at the time of retirement — if not before.

A Personal Rationale for the Founder. The transfer zone in leadership succession is often particularly painful. The process requires trust between the founder and the successor. Both must be committed to success. The founder must be enthusiastic about passing on the business. And the successor must be deserving of authority.

Even with all these ingredients present, the parent may go through a grieving period. The son or daughter may also suffer pain, perhaps because of disagreements over power, money or the successor's readiness to do the job.

Just as the successor needs a personal rationale, the founder must think through the reasons succession is worthwhile. "It's difficult now, but it's worth it because ....." the founder may reason, filling in the blanks with any number of important values, from "we employ a lot of people" to "I'm proud to have created an organization that can survive."

Sorting out your feelings will help you through this difficult time. Outside directors, trusted professional advisors or other peers can act as a catalyst, conscience or source of personal support in the letting-go process.

Post-Transition Roles for the Founder. Any relay runner who has been racing at top speed doesn't fall motionless after passing the baton.

He or she slows down gradually, sometimes encouraging the team or helping in other ways.

Similarly, **succession means the family-business founder must find a new role.** He or she is still part of the team and still eager for its success. But it is time for new responsibilities that match the founder's unique capabilities and make the most of his or her name and reputation.

Whatever the role, it should entail functions that no one can perform better than the founder.

Some former CEOs manage a part of the family business that has been spun off under their control. Others continue to perform a specific function within the business that they enjoy. The retired former owner of a Midwestern printing concern loves the production end of the business, so he visits printing plants and equipment shows for current management and evaluates prospective new manufacturing sites.

Some assume a "cultural ombudsman" role. This person communicates corporate values and traditions to employees and others, then listens to and relays to management any exceptions to that culture. The owner of a Midwestern chemical concern, after giving all his stock to his four children in a phased transaction, chose this role for himself. Acting as a kind of "corporate conscience," he circulated among employees, listening and taking an interest in what they were doing. He also wrote the company newsletter. In the process, this entrepreneur was able to transmit invaluable experience and a profound pride and confidence in the future of the business.

Some founders write a history of the business. Others do external public relations, acting as a sort of "chief ambassadorial officer" — a visible symbol of the company and its most important relationships and traditions. The founder of one family-owned food business finances and publicizes public-service research on nutrition. Another visits all his company's sales forces and key customers and manages the company's float in the Rose Bowl parade.

Some become active in trade groups as industry spokespersons. Others assist in employee training or in relations with lenders. Still others jump into politics or public service, promoting the business indirectly by enhancing the family name and reputation.

Some retiring CEOs strike out in an entirely new direction, starting a new business or a foundation.

Whatever the endeavor, it should be as exciting and creative as the venture left behind.

Communicating the Decision. The way the succession decisio
communicated to the family and the company can have a big impact on
the outcome.

If other family members or key managers think that one candidate was
pulled out of the pack just because he or she was Mom or Dad's favorite, that successor will lack credibility and authority from the start.

On the other hand, **if it is clear to everyone involved that the successor survived a planned selection process based on objective criteria, the transition is likely to go more smoothly.** This means that com-
munication with the family about succession should begin as soon as
possible, often before any candidates have been identified.

Once a choice is made, the decision should be conveyed with sensi-
tivity to both the family and the needs of the business. The message
shouldn't leave most of the family feeling inferior to the person chosen.
On the other hand, it should leave no room for doubt that the successor
is capable, in control and honored.

Most family businesses say too little about the succession decision for
fear of offending someone. The result is that no one assigns much importance to the shift in authority. This can undermine the successor.

Once succession plans are firm, the founder should make clear pub-
licly that he or she intends to retire. The company's mission, strategy and
values should be expressed at the same time, along with key elements
of the succession plan.

When the baton is passed, the founder and successor should prepare
a joint statement to the company that articulates again the business's ob-
jectives and strategy and describes all shifts in responsibility. Some statement about the founder's post-retirement plans should be part of this
announcement, particularly if he or she continues to play any role in
relation to the business. This leaves no room for confusion or, worse,
for the return of the founder.

The Successor's Role. Successors face a special communications challenge. In the unique world of family business, each new generation of
management needs to rediscover for itself the meaning in ownership and
find new ways to articulate it.

Successors should try above all to communicate commitment to the
enterprise and to the family. They need not — and should not — pretend
to be the founder. But they can make great strides toward effective leadership by expressing similar passion and enthusiasm for the business in
their own distinct way.

When Steve Forbes, successor to Malcolm Forbes as head of the

Forbes publishing empire, took over after his father's death, he didn't pretend to become his flamboyant father.

"Many have asked ... aren't you worried that the firm will be hurt by the fact you seem to lack your father's attention getting style?" Steve Forbes wrote in his inaugural *Forbes* issue as chief executive.

"Pop would be very disappointed if I tried to imitate him," he wrote. "'I have my own way of doing things, and, in time, you will develop yours,' he told me more than 20 years ago. 'Don't try to be what you're not.'

"So while styles may change, the spirit that animates this magazine and our other enterprises will remain constant. My father and I shared a similarly intense love for this business."

Steve added, "There is no replacing my father, but I bring the same spirit of dedication and joy to the job that he did ..."

Perhaps most important, **the effective successor sees stewardship of the family's assets as a privilege.** For many years, Malcolm Forbes had told family members that he intended to give Steve both management and ownership control. "As one said to me, 'Don't blow our inheritance.' In my interest and theirs — I will work to increase it," Steve wrote.

Once the leadership transition is complete, an era passes for both founder and successor and some sadness may ensue. But for the family and the business as a whole, the transfer of the baton is a new milestone on the path to continuity.

Organizational Succession. Family business owners often think of succession planning only in terms of the business's leadership.

But **succession brings profound change to the entire organization.** New career paths for other key executives, changes in the corporate culture, new management systems and styles — all can bring tremendous stress. Briefly, here are some critical aspects of planning for organizational succession.

The Management Team. The new management team must be developed in a way that will support the successor, but this process should be handled carefully. The succession plan should describe the successor's opportunities to

> **"There is no replacing my father, but I bring the same spirit of dedication and joy to the job that he did."**
>
> **- Malcolm Forbes, Jr.**

make changes in top management — an area than can be especially sensitive for the departing CEO.

Will longtime loyal executives be retained? Are any positions redundant with those held by the successor's chosen team? These questions can stir competitive feelings between parents and offspring.

Also, makeup of the board may need to be altered to meet the needs of the new CEO. This too should be discussed in the succession plan, to avoid misunderstandings or hard feelings.

Other Important Family and Non-Family Employees. Just as the successor's career path has been well-defined, other family members' opportunities should be charted too. Siblings or cousins need a clear, planned course of development under the new CEO.

Career, compensation and performance-review plans should be laid for key family and non-family managers who were not chosen as successors. A participation policy for family members in the business, covering entry and exit from family-business jobs, part-time work, the role of in-laws and so on, should be made clear.

Some companies include in their succession plans a set of rules governing family members' working relationships. Exhibit 4 contains an example of one company's position on this issue.

Accountability. A performance-review plan for the successor is crucial. The new CEO needs feedback, and shareholders need to know that he or she will be held accountable.

EXHIBIT 4 ██

One Company's Rules on Family Working Relationships

As part of the career planning discussions, we can explore several "rules of thumb" for relatives working together. For example, many believe it best if:

- family members don't report to one another;
- family members seek separate areas of interest, involving different divisions or functions;
- family members avoid following each other in job progressions to allow some self-identity.

Shareholder Relations. The founder's retirement also creates a need for a new family leader — someone who focuses on managing family traditions and communications. This role is particularly important as ownership expands to more shareholders in succeeding generations. The successor may take this responsibility, or it may fall to another family member. Either way, the responsibility should be clearly accepted by someone.

Some family businesses embrace policies guiding shareholder communications. Here is an excerpt from one company's statement:

> "It's important that the entire family be aware of general expectations, succession plans and arrangements with individual family members. Compensation, benefits and perquisites are best an open book.
>
> **"It's also important that inactive shareholders understand the demanding requirements and burdens of leadership.** These are most usually under-appreciated. Career planning may seem like a special privilege, but it is essential for the strength of the company and common to all well-run companies. Informal discussions between the Board and the shareholders can clarify any questions or misunderstandings."

As mentioned above, this is also the time to **develop new buy-sell agreements between shareholders and new estate plans.** Any existing agreements probably covered transactions between the founder and the company to protect the leader's spouse in the event of death. Now, the next generation of owners, usually co-owning siblings or cousins, need agreements that suit the new ownership structure.

Understanding Family Tensions

Succession planning in families with multiple children is a delicate task that breeds conflict. It can be frustrating for everyone involved.

Many families make the mistake, for instance, of assuming that all members share the same value system. In fact, siblings may have sharply different value systems. Birth order can have a big impact. So can birth dates. A firstborn might be raised by hard-pressed parents who are working night and day. By the time the fourth offspring reaches childhood, the same parents may be affluent and easing into retirement. So even though siblings have grown up in the same family, they may approach life as if they had been raised by different parents.

Rivalry among siblings often intensifies in the family business. While it can motivate siblings to turn in excellent job performances, competition also can career out of control, sparking divisive battles that hurt the company.

Whether they like it or not, family-business siblings also find themselves harnessed with their brothers and sisters in the most fragile of business relationships — the partnership. The *MBA Dictionary* defines partnership as "a merchant vessel prone to collision with other vessels, especially friendships." If partnerships tend to sink friendships, imagine their impact on sibling relationships!

Children's spouses introduce another source of conflict. Spouses often don't know the family business well. When their husbands and wives return home each night, they typically hear only about the problems at work, not the joys. Also, spouses may grow jealous over seeming inequities in family members' pay and perks. As a result, even innocent in-laws may over time tend to pull the family apart.

Role conflict is another cause of strain. Siblings easily grow to resent playing professional roles in relation to each other. "I hate to demand deadlines from my brother or ask embarrassing questions in staff meetings," one brother might say. "I can manage him, but I hate to go through that."

The other brother likely has a different view: "Why do I have to report back to my brother? Doesn't he trust me to know that I got the job done?"

Whatever the problem, you're not alone; thousands of other family-business owners are experiencing the same thing. An outside board or professional advisor can often be helpful in defusing conflict. While we won't discuss managing these issues at length here, Table 5 contains

TABLE 5

TIPS FOR PEACEFUL CO-OWNERSHIP AND CO-MANAGEMENT

- Give top priority to the best interests of the business.
- Set up separate areas of responsibility.
- Spend some time away from each other.
- Respect each other's areas of special interest.
- Speak each other's language.
- Hold annual airing-out sessions.
- Keep attitudes toward each other healthy and constructive.
- Agree on a system of compensation and perks.
- Meet informally sometimes just to talk.
- Develop a code or pledge of conduct with respect to each other.
- Arrange for a common office area shared by siblings.
- Develop a mission statement for the partnership.

a few ideas other family businesses have found helpful.

Sometimes, getting along goes back to the basic rules of childhood. When the members of one four-sibling partnership were asked why their business relationship had worked so well, they had a short answer: "Our parents taught us to trust each other."

A little empathy for other family members can leaven difficult moments. No matter how frustrating the children's role in succession, for instance, parents also have a difficult job. How can parents make a choice among children they love equally? How can parents reconcile their role as discriminating managers with their role as parents who value and love their children unconditionally? When are they to act like parents, and when like managers?

Clearly, parents face a fundamental dilemma in managing family-business succession.

"Our parents taught us to trust each other."

Other Pitfalls: Where Are You Most Likely to Stumble?

Some pitfalls of succession planning have already been mentioned. But a few are so common that they deserve a closer look.

No Safety Net. An Achilles heel common in even the most polished succession campaigns is the failure to plan for Mom and Dad's personal financial security.

Parents need to know that their future is clear financially (preferably independent of the business) and that their estate plans are in order before they can give up control gracefully. And successors need to know that their parents' well-being can't be jeopardized by any management risk they may take.

Once succession is complete, **parents should be able to sustain their standard of living indefinitely without relying on their children or the business.** Without this security net, a destructive dynamic can develop that saps the momentum of the business: Parents may worry silently that their kids aren't more entrepreneurial and inclined to take risks in managing the business. And the children may grow increasingly risk-averse because they're worried about their parents' financial security.

As this dynamic shows, succession planning in the family business is like an equation. A family can't complete a good succession plan unless the parents' estate and personal financial plans are in order. Estate planning can't be conducted without succession plans for management and ownership. As mentioned earlier, two other key plans — a family statement of mission and a strategic plan — are crucial to this equation too.

Selecting the Wrong Successor. If succession is the ultimate management challenge, it also may be the ultimate test of a CEO's self-knowledge. Many well-meaning CEOs botch the succession process because they unintentionally select a successor who will fail. In a 1974 article in the *Harvard Business Review,* Harry Levinson cited several reasons:

- The incumbent may be blinded by hindsight, oblivious to the changing conditions that dictate a new role for the organization's next leader.

- The CEO may not recognize qualities in him or herself that lead to success, and therefore won't seek them in others.

- The CEO may be blinded by an unconscious rivalry with the successor.

- The CEO may be so committed to tradition that he or she automatically rules out innovators or outsiders.

Setting the Kids Up to Fail. Some founders, in an unconscious attempt to prove they are indispensable, actually sabotage their successors without realizing it.

"This business is nothing without me," one founder said as he prepared to retire and hand control over to his son. "It takes a lot of capital to run this business. But there's no way I would leave enough money in the business for my son to succeed, because he'd just blow it."

One problem was that the father didn't trust his son. But a deeper impulse was to prove that he was essential — to have the last word ("I told you it would never work without me") and, in a perverse way, to prolong his presence in the business even after he had retired.

In his own negative way, this founder is trying to achieve immortality. But the result will be destructive for everyone concerned.

Shareholder Conflict. Another pitfall is the potential for conflict between passive shareholders and those who are active in the business.

As the business passes to the second, but especially to the third or fourth, generations of family ownership, the interests of these two groups diverge. **Passive shareholders may begin to see the business as a birthright,** and they resent the pay and perks of family members who are working in the business. Also, active holders may resent passive owners' demands for dividends and liquidity.

This problem is worsened by the fact that the small to medium-sized family business must grow very fast to support multiple offspring in the same style as their parents. Resentments over having to settle for dwindling shares of the same pie can flare into destructive family clashes that drain the business.

In large businesses with many family shareholders, these problems can often be managed as if in a public company. Shareholder meetings and formation of a family council become vehicles for finding consensus and defining the proper role of passive owners.

But in family businesses with only a few holders, ownership and management should be kept in the same hands. This requires some work on writing buy-sell agreements and securing cash to buy out passive holders. But it can pay big dividends in the form of peaceful growth for the business.

Parental Impasse. Sometimes family-business founders simply find it too difficult to address important aspects of succession planning. This may leave the younger generation stalled, wondering, "How am I ever going to get anything going around here?"

Sometimes, peers of the parent can help him or her face the need. A successor might ask a respected lawyer, accountant, or other advisor with a secure relationship with the founder: "I don't want to sound too pushy, but isn't it unusual that we have no stock-transfer plan? Could you talk to my father about this?" This trusted peer may be able to bring up the issue in a way the founder can tolerate.

Third parties should never be used just as sounding boards, however. Venting one's frustration on Mom or another family member or friend in hopes of finding an ally only creates triangles that can block a constructive, peaceful solution.

Conclusion

Preparing to pass the family business on to the next generation is perhaps the toughest and most critical challenge facing the business owner.

But succession planning also poses a unique opportunity to perpetuate the privileges and rewards of private ownership. Before beginning the process in earnest, business owners should prepare estate, strategic and family-mission plans as a foundation for succession. Then, a specific succession plan, including the process for choosing a successor, should be laid.

Once a potential successor or successors have been developed and a choice has been made, leadership and ownership control of the business should be transferred in a step-by-step process that allows both founder and successor to assume their new roles smoothly and with a minimum of pain and disruption. Finally, the founder should devote time and thought to preparing for a secure retirement, plotting activities that will be at least as creative and exciting as those he or she has left behind.

Succession is often the most painful stage in the life cycle of the family business. Yet **many owners find great reward in perpetuating an organization that will foster a strong family identity and perpetuate the family's values, goals and well-being long after the founder is gone.**

Index

41

The Authors

Craig E. Aronoff and John L. Ward have long been recognized as leaders in the family business field. Founding principals of the **Family Business Consulting Group**, they work with hundreds of family businesses around the world. Recipients of the Family Firm Institute's Beckhard Award for outstanding contributions to family business practice, they have spoken to family business audiences on every continent. Their books include *Family Business Sourcebook II* and the three-volume series, *The Future of Private Enterprise.*

Craig E. Aronoff, Ph.D., holds the Dinos Eminent Scholar Chair of Private Enterprise and is professor of management at Kennesaw State University (Atlanta). He founded and directs the university's Cox Family Enterprise Center. The center focuses on education and research for family businesses, and its programs have been emulated by more than 100 universities worldwide. In addition to his under-graduate degree from Northwestern University and Masters from the University of Pennsylvania, he holds a Ph.D. in organizational com-munication from the University of Texas.

John L. Ward, Ph.D., is Clinical Professor of Family Enterprises at Northwestern University's Kellogg Graduate School of Manage-ment. He is a regular visiting lecturer at two European business schools. He has also previously been associate dean of Loyola Uni-versity Chicago's Graduate School of Business, and a senior associ-ate with Strategic Planning Institute (PIMS Program) in Cambridge, Massachusetts. A graduate of Northwestern University (B.A) and Stanford Graduate School of Business (M.B.A. and Ph.D.), his *Keep-ing the Family Business Healthy* and *Creating Effective Boards for Private Enterprises* are leading books in the family business field.

The best information resources for business-owning families and their advisors

The Family Business Leadership Series
Concise guides dealing with the most pressing challenges and significant opportunities confronting family businesses.

Comprehensive — Readable — Thoroughly Practical
- *Family Meetings: How to Build a Stronger Family and a Stronger Business*
- *Another Kind of Hero: Preparing Successors for Leadership*
- *How Families Work Together*
- *Family Business Compensation*
- *How to Choose & Use Advisors: Getting the Best Professional Family Business Advice*
- *Financing Transitions: Managing Capital and Liquidity in the Family Business*
- *Family Business Governance: Maximizing Family and Business Potential*
- *Preparing Your Family Business for Strategic Change*
- *Making Sibling Teams Work: The Next Generation*
- *Developing Family Business Policies: Your Guide to the Future*
- *Family Business Values: How to Assure a Legacy of Continuity and Success*
- *More Than Family: Non-Family Executives in the Family Business*
- New guides on critical issues published every six to twelve months

The Family Business ADVISOR Monthly Newsletter

Family Business Sourcebook II
Edited by Drs. Aronoff and Ward with Dr. Joseph H. Astrachan, *Family Business Sourcebook II* contains the best thoughts, advice, experience and insights on the subject of family business. Virtually all of the best-known experts in the field are represented.

Now Available:
John Ward's Groundbreaking Family Business Classics
- *Keeping The Family Business Healthy*
- *Creating Effective Boards For Private Enterprises*

For more information:
Business Owner Resources, P.O. Box 4356, Marietta, GA 30061
Tel: 800-551-0633 or 770-425-6673